WORLD WAR II CHRONICLES

AIR WAR!

DWIGHT JON ZIMMERMAN,
MILITARY HISTORY CONSULTANT

BY JULIE KLAM

Published by Smart Apple Media, 1980 Lookout Drive, North Mankato, Minnesota 56003

Produced by Byron Preiss Visual Publications, Inc.

Library of Congress Cataloging-in-Publication Data

Klam, Julie.

Air war! / by Julie Klam.

v. cm. — (World War II chronicles; bk. 3)

Contents: Pt. 1. Air war in Europe. The new generation of fighters and bombers — Blitzkrieg — The Battle of France — The Battle
of Britain — Pilots: the early years — Pilots: the U.S. Army Air Force in the European theater of operations — The Mediterranean
air war: North Africa, Sicily, Italy — Air attack on German war industries — American bombers and fighters in Europe — The
Schweinfurt raids — Air power for D-Day — The bombing of Dresden — Germany's jet-powered weapons. Contents: Pt. 2. Air war
in the Pacific. Pearl Harbor — The Flying Tigers — Aircraft carriers — Navy warplanes — Battle of Midway — U. S. Navy and
Marine aces in the Pacific — Island-hopping strategy — The Marianas Turkey Shoot — B-29 Superfortress — U. S. Army Air Force
aces in the Pacific — Kamikazes — Atomic bombs on Hiroshima and Nagasaki by the Enola Gay and Bock's Car.

ISBN 1-58340-189-X

1. World War, 1939-1945—Aerial operations—Juvenile literature. [1. World War, 1939-1945—Aerial operations.] I. Title.

D785 .K53 2002

940.54'49—dc21   2002017648

First Edition

2 4 6 8 9 7 5 3 1

CONTENTS:

INTRODUCTION

✚ (opposite): Adolf Hitler addresses the Reichstag.

✚ Benito Mussolini

✚ Hirohito

World War II was the greatest conflict of the 20th century. Fought on every continent except Antarctica and across every ocean, it was truly a "world war." Like many other wars, over time it evolved. Modern technology and strategic advancements changed the rules of combat forever, allowing for widespread attacks from the air, the ground, and the sea.

For the Chinese, the war began in 1931, when Japan invaded northeastern China. When Germany invaded Poland in 1939, Europeans were dragged into the fray. Americans did not enter World War II until December 7, 1941, when Japan attacked Pearl Harbor, Hawaii.

World War II pitted two sides against each other, the Axis powers and the Allied countries. The main Axis nations were Germany, Japan, and Italy. The Axis powers were led by Chancellor Adolf Hitler, the head of the Nazi Party in Germany; Premier Benito Mussolini, the head of the Fascists in Italy; and Japan's Emperor Hirohito and the military government headed by Prime Minister Hideki Tojo. The Allies included Britain, France, the Soviet Union, China, and the United States. The leaders of the Allies were Britain's Prime

Minister Winston Churchill, who had replaced Neville Chamberlain in 1940; General Charles de Gaulle of France; the Soviet Union's Marshal Josef Stalin; China's Generalissimo Chiang Kai-shek; and Franklin Delano Roosevelt, the president of the United States. The two sides clashed primarily in the Pacific Ocean and Asia, which Japan sought to control, and in the Atlantic Ocean, Europe, and North Africa, where Germany and Italy were trying to take over.

World War II finally ended in 1945, first in Europe on May 8, with Germany's total capitulation. Then, on September 2, the Japanese signed the document for their unconditional surrender after the United States had dropped two atomic bombs on Japan. World War II left 50 million people dead and millions of others wounded, both physically and mentally.

The war encompassed the feats of extraordinary heroes and the worst villains imaginable, with thrilling triumphs and heartrending tragedies. *Air War!* presents aviation's important role in the battles of World War II, from the "gallant few" lionized by Winston Churchill after the German blitzkrieg to the Allied squadrons that swept the skies clear of Axis aircraft to the aviators who dropped the atomic bombs on Japan.

✛ Josef Stalin

✛ Chiang Kai-shek

✛ (right): Franklin Delano Roosevelt

Map of German Conquests

- Germany (1939)
- Axis Occupied Territory (1942)
- Italy and Its Territories
- Treaty with Axis
- Allied Powers
- Allied Protectorates
- Neutral Countries
- Vichy France and Territories

FINLAND

NORWAY

SWEDEN

ESTONIA

North Sea

Baltic Sea

LATVIA

LITHUANIA

UNION OF SOVIET SOCIALIST REPUBLICS

IRELAND

UNITED KINGDOM

DENMARK

EAST PRUSSIA

THE NETHERLANDS

BELGIUM

GERMANY

POLAND

Atlantic Ocean

LUXEMBOURG

FRANCE

SLOVAKIA

SWITZERLAND

HUNGARY

VICHY FRANCE

YUGOSLAVIA

ROMANIA

Black Sea

Adriatic Sea

PORTUGAL

SPAIN

ITALY

BULGARIA

ALBANIA

TURKEY

GREECE

SYRIA

SPANISH MOROCCO

IRAQ

MOROCCO

Mediterranean Sea

PALESTINE

TRANS-JORDAN

TUNISIA

ALGERIA

LIBYA

EGYPT

SAUDI ARABIA

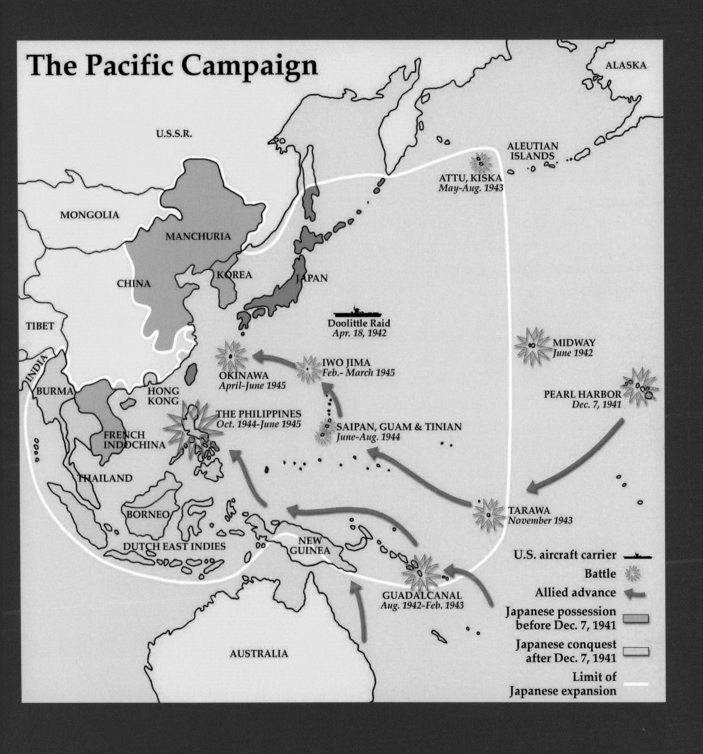

The Pacific Campaign

ALASKA

U.S.S.R.

MONGOLIA

MANCHURIA

CHINA

KOREA

JAPAN

TIBET

INDIA

BURMA

HONG KONG

FRENCH INDOCHINA

THAILAND

BORNEO

DUTCH EAST INDIES

NEW GUINEA

AUSTRALIA

ALEUTIAN ISLANDS

ATTU, KISKA
May-Aug. 1943

Doolittle Raid
Apr. 18, 1942

MIDWAY
June 1942

OKINAWA
April-June 1945

IWO JIMA
Feb.- March 1945

PEARL HARBOR
Dec. 7, 1941

THE PHILIPPINES
Oct. 1944-June 1945

SAIPAN, GUAM & TINIAN
June-Aug. 1944

TARAWA
November 1943

GUADALCANAL
Aug. 1942-Feb. 1943

U.S. aircraft carrier

Battle

Allied advance

Japanese possession before Dec. 7, 1941

Japanese conquest after Dec. 7, 1941

Limit of Japanese expansion

In the years leading up to World War II, leaders on both sides saw that airplanes would be important weapons. Germany was the first country to successfully use air power as a tactical weapon designed to support its armies in its new form of warfare, the blitzkrieg, a swift form of attack that relies on the shock value of the speed and power of tanks and airplanes to defeat an enemy army. Great Britain was the first country to develop air power into a strategic weapon designed to destroy an enemy's war industries. In the early years of the war, the only way that Britain, an island country, could strike back at Germany was through the air with its Royal Air Force (RAF). Britain manufactured bombers to do this. One type, the Stirling, could fly as far as 2,000 miles (3,219 km) without refueling and drop up to 14,000 pounds (6,350 kg) of bombs on German cities and war-production industrial centers. To keep their own losses low, British crews were trained to conduct their missions at night. Later, when

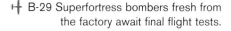 B-29 Superfortress bombers fresh from the factory await final flight tests.

A tired B-17 crew leaving their bomber, having completed another mission.

the United States entered the war, the two countries organized around-the-clock bombing of Axis targets, with the United States attacking during the day with its B-17 Flying Fortresses and B-24 Liberators, and the British taking over at nightfall.

Against Japan, the United States needed a bomber that could fly vast distances over the Pacific Ocean. America created the awesome B-29 Superfortress, a heavy bomber that could carry a 20,000-pound (9,072 kg) payload of bombs up to 3,700 miles (5,955 km) one way—the distance from Juneau, Alaska, to Miami, Florida, and then some!

These, and many other airplanes and their pilots and crews, would battle for control of the skies over Europe, Africa, Asia, and the Pacific.

Hitler was a veteran of World War I. He refused to make the same mistakes that had caused the German high command to get bogged down in the static trench warfare that ultimately led to Germany's defeat. Hitler ordered his military leaders to develop a new style of warfare—one that would combine the power of tanks, motorized infantry, and aircraft to boldly strike with all the speed and power of a lightning bolt. Hitler called this new type of warfare "blitzkrieg," which means "lightning war."

⊬ A German He-111 (Heinkel) bomber drops bombs on a target on the Russian front.

One of the key elements in Hitler's blitzkrieg was the use of the German air force, the Luftwaffe. Led by Reich Marshal Hermann Goering, a former World War I fighter ace and the second-most powerful man in Germany after Hitler, the Luftwaffe would attack the enemy first, thus making it easier for the German army to destroy it. One of the most terrifying aircraft in the Luftwaffe's arsenal was the Junkers Ju-87 Sturzkampfflugzeug, or Stuka dive-bomber. When it began its attack, high-pitched siren "screamers" attached to its landing gear would emit a howl that struck fear into the hearts of soldiers and civilians alike.

Germany's first full-scale demonstration of blitzkrieg was the invasion of Poland on September 1, 1939. The Luftwaffe struck first, destroying targets at will and provoking terror with the banshee-wailing Stukas. The German armored forces—the Panzers—swiftly followed, punching deep holes in the confused Polish army ranks. Into these breaches poured the German infantry. In less than a month, Poland was defeated and forced to surrender.

THE BATTLE OF FRANCE

Though Great Britain and France had declared war on Germany after its attack on Poland, the two nations did not promptly attack Germany. Instead, the leaders of Britain and France decided to wait and see what the Germans did first. The French commanders were content to believe that the fortifications of the Maginot Line (a massive system of cannons, machine guns, trenches, barbed wire, and other defenses that stretched along the French-German border from Switzerland to Belgium) were impenetrable. Also, Great Britain was not powerful enough to launch an attack on its own. This standoff situation was called the "Phony War" in America, the *Sitzkrieg* ("sit-down war") in England, and *la drôle de guerre* ("the funny war") in France. But while Great Britain and France waited, Hitler used the time to prepare for his next attack.

The false peace of the Phony War was broken by the German invasion of Denmark and Norway in April 1940. This was a prelude to Hitler's main effort, his most ambitious campaign to date: the Battle of France.

On May 10, 1940, Hitler shocked Britain and France by attacking through the neutral countries of the Netherlands, Belgium, and Luxembourg—completely bypassing the Maginot Line. In less than six weeks, France surrendered. Only one European power remained to be conquered, the defiant, but terribly weakened, Great Britain.

✠ France surrenders to Germany at Compiègne, June 22, 1940, inside the same railroad car the Germans had surrendered to the Allies in at the end of World War I.

THE BATTLE OF BRITAIN

In the summer of 1940, Hitler was the master of Europe. Only the island nation of Great Britain remained defiantly free of Nazi control. To conquer Great Britain, Hitler decided that his armies would have to sail across the English Channel, an invasion plan entitled Operation Sealion. But first, Germany would have to control the skies over southern England, where the proposed landing sites for German troops were located. This meant that the Luftwaffe would have to destroy Britain's Royal Air Force (RAF). Reich Marshal Hermann Goering looked forward to this with great pleasure. A braggart and a bully, Goering boasted that his Luftwaffe would quickly destroy the RAF.

The Battle of Britain began in mid-June and lasted until mid-September 1940. Huge squadrons of Luftwaffe fighters and bombers blackened the daytime skies over England. But, despite repeated attacks, the Luftwaffe failed to defeat the RAF. Though Luftwaffe attacks continued until June 1941, when Germany attacked the Soviet Union, the Battle of Britain was effectively won by the British in mid-September 1940, and Operation Sealion was shelved. Prime Minister Churchill paid tribute to the RAF in a speech saying, "Never in the field of human conflict was so much owed by so many to so few."

✚ A fireman helps homeless people over rubble in Southampton, England, after a German bombing raid during the Battle of Britain, December 1940.

PILOTS: U.S. ARMY AIR FORCE IN THE EUROPEAN THEATER OF OPERATIONS

Here is one of the great American aces in the European Theater of Operations and a famous squadron that fought against the Germans.

Captain Robert S. Johnson

One top U.S. Army Air Force ace was Captain Robert S. Johnson, who scored 27 confirmed victories. Captain Johnson flew the P-47 Thunderbolt, considered the toughest fighter plane in the USAAF. Johnson proved that on one harrowing mission. After he finally managed to get his shot-up plane home, he assessed the damage:

I'm still standing in one place when my count of the bullet holes reaches past a hundred. . . . Every square foot, it seems, is covered with holes. There are five holes in the propeller. . . . Five cannon shell holes [are] in the right wing; four [are] in the left wing. . . . Needless to say, she would never fly again.

Tuskegee Airmen: The 332nd Fighter Group

Another group of American pilot heroes was the 332nd Fighter Group, part of an all-African-American group known as the Tuskegee Airmen. "The Redtails"—so named because the tails of their P-51 Mustangs were painted bright red—fought both American prejudice and Nazi military might during World War II. The 332nd achieved an outstanding record during the war. But it was in their role as "Little Friends"—the term bomber crews used for the fighter planes that provided escort protection—that they achieved a statistic that stands head and shoulders above all others and made them unique among all fighter groups. The 332nd did not lose a single bomber that they escorted. It was a record no other fighter group in the USAAF matched.

✛ Benjamin O. Davis Jr., one of the "Redtail" pilots.

THE MEDITERRANEAN AIR WAR: NORTH AFRICA, SICILY, AND ITALY

In early 1943, soon after the successful Allied invasion and liberation of Morocco and Algeria, President Roosevelt and Prime Minister Churchill met in Casablanca, Morocco, to plan military strategy for the Allies. The decision was made to sweep the Germans out of the Mediterranean. They would start by invading the Italian island of Sicily and, later, mainland Italy.

Operation Husky, the invasion of Sicily, was launched in July 1943. It was the first time that the British and the Americans put into widespread practice the lessons learned from Germany's use of paratroopers in the conquest of Belgium (1940) and Crete (1941). The Allies' actions permanently expanded the definition of air power beyond fighters and bombers. Both the British and the American forces used two types of airborne troops. One was paratroopers, who leaped out of transport planes and parachuted to the ground. The second was soldiers who were carried to the battlefield in special gliders. The American Seventh Army, led by General George S. Patton Jr., used an airborne task force on the night of the invasion to capture the high ground just beyond the Seventh Army's landing sites.

✛ George S. Patton gives orders to troops in Sicily.

+ Allied leaders, including George S. Patton, center, inspect an invasion force.

Many problems occurred during the invasion. High winds blew many airplanes and gliders off course. And there were accidents because so many crews were inexperienced. But enough paratroopers successfully landed in Sicily to disrupt the enemy's attempts to defeat the Allied invasion force. The lessons learned in Operation Husky would be invaluable when the Allies began making plans for Operation Overlord, the invasion of France.

Once the Allies had liberated Sicily in 1943, they next launched the invasion of mainland Italy. The battle up the boot of Italy proved to be long and hard. The Germans built strong defenses and fought tenaciously over every foot of ground. Chronic bad weather often inhibited Allied air power from helping break the deadlock.

One particularly strong German defense was around the Benedictine monastery of Monte Cassino. Allied high command decided that the only way to break the German defenses was to stage a huge bombing campaign of the monastery. More than 250 American bombers attacked Monte Cassino, destroying the monastery and cloisters. German troops moved into the shattered remains and used the ruins to make even stronger defenses. As a result, the Allied troops had to fight even harder to conquer Monte Cassino.

The Allies kept the pressure on the Germans. Though the fighting was difficult, by the end of the war in Europe in May 1945, the Allies had successfully liberated almost all of Italy.

✝ In Naples, Italy, a boy helps his friend, mutilated in the war, across the street.

TARGET: GERMAN WAR INDUSTRIES

Allied air raids on Germany began with small RAF raids of only a few planes on German cities near the Dutch and Belgian borders. On May 30, 1942, RAF's Bomber Command was strong enough to launch its first 1,000-plane raid of a German city. The target was Cologne, on the Rhine River. The giant raid caused widespread destruction to both civilian property and industrial areas.

Allied forces hoped strategic bombing could help them win the war, with bombers capable of carrying heavy loads and the ability to drop them with bull's-eye precision. But, despite horrendous damage, German industrial output actually increased as the war continued. The only area in which strategic bombing made a lasting impact was in the destruction of Germany's natural and synthetic oil refineries.

AMERICAN BOMBERS AND FIGHTERS IN EUROPE

American pilots flew some of the greatest warplanes in the world. In Europe those planes were:

B-17 Flying Fortress

One of the most famous bombers of all time was the B-17. With up to 13 machine guns, the B-17 seemed to be a genuine flying "fortress in the sky." It could drop a 6,000-pound (2,722 kg) payload of bombs on targets up to 2,000 miles (3,219 km) away. The B-17 could also sustain incredible damage and remain airborne. As B-17 pilot Lieutenant Raymond W. Wild of the 92nd Bomb Group said:

Boy, did it take punishment. It would fly when it shouldn't fly . . . Everybody in the '17 knew that the plane would get back. If they could stay in it, and stay alive, they knew they'd get back. We all had tremendous confidence in the airplane.

B-24 Liberator

More Liberators were built than any other U.S. plane during World War II. It could carry an 8,000-pound (2,629 kg) bomb load more than 2,000 miles (3,219 km). Chunky and slab-sided,

✛ B-24 Liberators fly home after a raid on the Ploesti oil refineries, May 1944.

the B-24 lacked the glamour and grace of the B-17, but it performed on more operational war fronts for a longer period and with a greater versatility than the more famous B-17. The B-24's most famous raid was the attack on the German-held oil refineries at Ploesti, Romania.

P-38 Lightning

The twin-engine Lightning had a revolutionary design for an interceptor. The Lightning proved to be the most versatile fighter of the war, serving on nearly all fronts and in every function, from long-distance, high-altitude photo reconnaissance to night fighting. The top two American aces in the war, Majors Richard Bong and Tommy McGuire, flew Lightnings.

P-47 Thunderbolt

Even the pilots who loved the Thunderbolt agreed that it was heavy and ugly. But it was the most rugged fighter in the war, as Captain Robert Johnson discovered after a German attack left his Thunderbolt riddled with holes but still able to fly him to his home base. It could also carry an incredible number of weapons and bombs, making it an ideal ground-attack aircraft as well.

P-51 Mustang

The Mustang was the most famous American fighter of World War II and was the fighter credited with dealing the Luftwaffe its death blow. The Mustang carried another distinction: It was a true Allied aircraft, for the American fighter was powered by a British Rolls-Royce Merlin engine.

B-17 Flying Fortresses attack from the sky over Europe.

THE SCHWEINFURT RAIDS

By early 1943, American air power had become a significant force in the war against Germany. Around-the-clock bombing, with the RAF attacking targets at night and the USAAF attacking the same targets during the day, was quickly becoming a common practice.

The top air commanders decided to unleash their air power on strategic targets deep within Germany that earlier had been beyond their reach.

The first of these long-distance strategic targets was the ball-bearing industry at Schweinfurt, less than 150 miles (241 km) northwest of Munich. Many military weapons, especially tanks and aircraft, needed ball bearings. One airplane alone needed more than 1,000 anti-friction bearings. Strategists believed that if they could knock out the Schweinfurt plants, they could deliver a long-term blow to Germany's war-making ability.

The plants were regarded as being so important that two raids were planned. The first was launched on August 17, 1943. The USAAF sent 230 bombers to Schweinfurt and suffered 25 percent losses—an appalling figure. Acceptable losses are less than 10 percent. The second raid, on Thursday, October 14, 1943, became known as Black Thursday because losses were just as devastating. In fact, losses due to the tough German defenses were so high that long-distance attacks were suspended until the Big Week operation—a six-day air offensive against the German fighter-manufacturing plants that took place in February 1944.

✛ A B-17 Flying Fortress shows damage from a German rocket, July 1943.

AIR POWER FOR D-DAY

In order to ensure the success of Operation Overlord, the invasion of Normandy, France (later and more famously known as D-Day), General Dwight Eisenhower, the supreme Allied commander in Europe, required help from the strategic-bomber commanders. He ordered them to strike all the railroad terminals, bridges, and ports across northern France, Belgium, and northwestern Germany. If successful, Eisenhower's "transportation plan" would prevent the Germans from being able to quickly send reinforcements to the landing sites.

Though the air commanders at first resisted, believing that their attacks on Germany's strategic industries such as oil and weapons manufacturing would produce better results, they ultimately agreed. For weeks leading up to the invasion, RAF and USAAF medium and heavy bombers repeatedly attacked every important transportation center

✈ P-51 Mustang fighters head home after a successful escort mission over Europe.

✠ Transport ships unload supplies on one of the D-Day beaches.

on their long list. The transportation plan worked. Thanks to the bombers, the Allies were able to secure the landing beaches at Normandy on June 6, 1944. And on D-Day, Allied air power not only provided an umbrella of air cover to defend the landing beaches, but it also carried paratroopers and troop-filled gliders.

THE BOMBING OF DRESDEN

By February 1945, it was obvious to everyone but the most fanatic Nazi that Germany was going to lose the war. The Soviet, British, and American armies had breached the German border in both the east and the west. The Allied Supreme Command stated that Dresden had become a major communications and transportation center in eastern Germany and, thus, was now considered to be a prime target for attack.

Before this, Dresden, considered one of the most beautiful cities in Europe because of its splendid architecture, had been bombed only once during the entire war. The British air command created a plan, Thunderclap, to flatten Dresden with a combination of high explosives and incendiary bombs. It began on the night of February 13, 1945, with 796 British Lancaster bombers dropping their payload on a city that had no anti-aircraft defenses. The following day, the USAAF attacked with more than 300 B-17 bombers. The resulting firestorm annihilated the beautiful center of Dresden.

✝ A cathedral statue overlooks the destruction of the center of Dresden, Germany.

Instead of bringing the war closer to an end, it caused a huge cry of outrage from the Nazi leaders, who used the attack as part of a propaganda campaign to strengthen the resolve of the German people.

GERMANY'S JET-POWERED WEAPONS

✚ A V-2 rocket

During World War II, Germany made an astonishing variety of deadly jet-powered weapons. These included a number of high-performance jet planes, the most famous being the Messerschmitt Me-262, and the V-1 flying bomb and V-2 rocket that were launched against London and other English cities.

When Allied pilots saw the Me-262 jets attack their bombers, even the bravest fighter pilot felt a touch of fear. With a top speed of 540 miles per hour (869 kmh), the Me-262 was about 100 miles an hour (161 kmh) faster than the fastest Allied fighter, the P-51 Mustang.

Because it had a maximum speed of about 420 miles per hour (676 kmh), the V-1 could be attacked and shot down by fighter planes. About half of the V-1 flying bombs launched at England were intercepted and destroyed. But nothing in the Allied arsenal could catch the V-2, which reached supersonic speeds of up to 3,600 miles per hour (5,794 kmh).

Fortunately for the Allies, all of these weapons became operational too late, in too small numbers, and were not used to their best advantage. Germany was defeated in May 1945.

PART II: AIR WAR IN THE PACIFIC

Pearl Harbor

The destructive capability of air power was devastatingly demonstrated to Americans by the pilots of the Imperial Japanese Navy on the morning of December 7, 1941, at Pearl Harbor, Hawaii.

Delivered without warning, the attack struck the island of Oahu in two waves, the first arriving just before 8 A.M. In addition to striking the U.S. Navy's port at Pearl Harbor, the Japanese fighter planes, dive-bombers, and torpedo bombers attacked the navy, Marine, and USAAF air fields as well. Two hours later, the victorious Japanese planes were gone. The damage they left behind was enormous.

✛ The Japanese sneak attack on December 7, 1941, demolished the Naval Air Station at Pearl Harbor.

Altogether, 18 capital ships were hit, including 8 battleships sunk or damaged. On the airfields, 164 warplanes were destroyed with almost an equal number damaged. The U.S. Navy's Pacific fleet had been decimated. Though the United States declared war on Japan the following day, thanks to the success of Japan's air power, the Japanese road to the conquest of Asia and the Pacific was now wide open.

NAVY WARPLANES

The U.S. Navy pilots in WWII were among the best trained in the world. That training was put to a severe test. Early in the war, the navy pilots flew warplanes that were in many ways inferior to the ones flown by their Japanese adversaries. Here are some of the more famous warplanes that the U.S. Navy pilots flew.

F-4F Wildcat

The Wildcat was the Navy's frontline fighter at the beginning of World War II. Though slower and less maneuverable than its main adversary, the Japanese Zero, it was more rugged, and with its six .50-caliber machine guns, it had more firepower than the Zero. The Wildcat participated in all the important naval battles in the first half of the war, including the Battle of the Coral Sea and Midway, until it was replaced by the F-6F Hellcat.

F-6F Hellcat

U.S. Navy pilots referred to the Hellcat as the "aluminum tank." Like its predecessor, the Wildcat, it carried tremendous firepower. In addition, it could be fitted with rockets and other munitions. More important, it could outperform the fast and maneuverable Zero in

 A Grumman Hellcat fighter prepares to take off.

a dogfight. The Hellcat's most spectacular success was in the aerial battle known as the Great Marianas Turkey Shoot, when the navy's Hellcats destroyed more than 160 Japanese aircraft in one day.

SBD Dauntless

The Dauntless was the navy's greatest dive-bomber during World War II. It saw action throughout the war. It achieved its greatest fame during the Battle of Midway in 1942, when its bombs destroyed four powerful Japanese fleet carriers in two days.

TBF Avenger

The Avenger was the navy's most successful torpedo bomber during World War II. Torpedo bombers were similar to dive-bombers. The biggest differences were in the way they attacked their targets and the types of explosives they carried. Dive-bombers attack from high altitudes (diving) and drop bombs that simply fall onto a target. Torpedo bombers make low-level attacks, flying straight and level just above the surface of the sea. When they get near their target, they release a motor-driven torpedo that drops into the sea and then propels itself toward the target.

Dauntless dive-bombers

Avenger torpedo bombers

THE FLYING TIGERS

In April 1941, the Chinese government, led by Chiang Kai-shek, agreed to let Claire Chennault, a retired officer from America's Army Air Force, colonel a squadron of American volunteer aviators in China's fight against Japan. About 100 pilots and 200 ground staff were recruited into the American Volunteer Group (A.V.G.) and equipped with three squadrons of P-40 Warhawk fighters. Though the Warhawk was in many ways outclassed by the faster and more maneuverable Japanese Zero, Chennault, who had studied Japanese tactics, taught his men aerial-combat tactics that exploited the strengths of their aircraft.

The A.V.G. came to be known as the Flying Tigers, after the distinctive eyes and bared-fang jaws painted on the noses of the fighters.

Before it was disbanded in 1942, after America had entered the war, the A.V.G. had achieved a record of 286 Japanese aircraft destroyed against losses of only 50 planes destroyed and 12 pilots killed.

One of the Flying Tiger pilots, Gregory "Pappy" Boyington, who had six victories as a member of the A.V.G., would go on to become a top Marine fighter ace and the leader of the famous Black Sheep squadron.

✠ A Chinese soldier stands guard over a line of American P-40 fighter planes from the Flying Tigers.

AIRCRAFT CARRIERS

For decades, the powerful battleship with its multiple batteries of large cannons and thick armored hull was considered the undisputed queen of the sea. All that changed on December 7, 1941, in the wreckage of Pearl Harbor. From that moment on, it was the aircraft carrier that would be the dominant warship.

An aircraft carrier could sail across the ocean, strike at targets more than 100 miles (161 km) from its position, and then sail in a different direction and, the next day, strike at another target hundreds of miles away.

Small escort carriers, which flew up to 36 obsolete planes, were used to support invasion landings and protect convoys from submarine attack. America's large fleet carriers, such as the *Yorktown*, the *Enterprise*, the *Essex*, and the *Wasp*, used mostly to destroy enemy fleets, carried a powerful strike force of up to 96 top-of-the-line planes each.

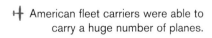
✠ American fleet carriers were able to carry a huge number of planes.

BATTLE OF MIDWAY

By the spring of 1942, the Japanese had conquered territory stretching from Burma almost to the middle of the Pacific Ocean. In order to solidify the control of their conquests, they needed to do two things. The first was to strengthen their ring of island defense outposts in the Central Pacific. The second was to destroy the U.S. aircraft carriers, the most important part of the U.S. fleet that had not been at Pearl Harbor when the Japanese had attacked on December 7, 1941. The top Japanese leaders, led by Admiral Isoroku Yamamoto, decided that an attack on the American-held island of Midway, located less than 1,200 miles (1,931 km) northwest of Pearl Harbor, would accomplish both goals.

Included in the plan to seize Midway was a landing of Japanese troops on Attu and Kiska, part of the Aleutian Islands chain of Alaska. By attacking Midway and the Aleutians, the Japanese would force the U.S. Navy aircraft carriers to do battle.

The primary attack on Midway would be delivered by a strike force composed of four large aircraft carriers, the *Akagi*, the *Kaga*, the *Hiryu*, and the *Soryu*, and their escorts of cruisers and destroyers. Against this force, the U.S. Navy could assemble a force of only three aircraft carriers, the *Enterprise*, the *Hornet*, and the *Yorktown*; eight cruisers; and a handful of destroyers. The *Yorktown* had been crippled from an earlier battle with a different Japanese fleet at the Battle of the Coral Sea north of Australia. But it was quickly made ready to fight in the Battle of Midway. To make matters even worse for the Americans, at this early stage in the war, the planes in the American arsenal were outclassed by those of the Japanese.

Though it would mean that the Japanese would hold the U.S. territory of Attu and Kiska, the American high command in the Pacific, led by Admiral Chester Nimitz, refused to attack the Japanese forces landing there and recognized that Midway was the main target. The Americans flew into battle on June 4, 1942. When the Battle of Midway was over on June 7, the Americans had sunk all four of the big Japanese carriers and one heavy cruiser, and destroyed more than 250 Japanese aircraft. American losses were one aircraft carrier, the *Yorktown*, and fewer than 150 aircraft. Thanks to the bravery and determination of the U.S. Navy pilots, the Japanese string of victories had been stopped.

U.S. NAVY AND MARINE ACES IN THE PACIFIC

There were many heroes in the air war in the Pacific. Here are just a couple of the outstanding aces from the U.S. Marine Corps and the U.S. Navy.

Commander David McCampbell

Commander McCampbell became the navy's top ace in the war, downing 34 Japanese aircraft. On one mission, flying with just one other navy pilot, McCampbell took on more than 40 Japanese warplanes that were attacking the U.S. fleet. Before the war ended, McCampbell was awarded the Medal of Honor, America's highest military decoration.

Major Gregory "Pappy" Boyington

The most colorful ace in the Marine Corps was Major Gregory Boyington, who started fighting the Japanese as a pilot for the Flying Tigers. After he transferred to the Marines, he was given a group of pilots who were considered misfits and poor fliers. Most people thought that not even he could whip those pilots into shape. But "Pappy" Boyington proved that in addition to being a top-notch fighter pilot, he was an excellent leader. He transformed that dispirited group into the successful Black Sheep squadron that was the terror of the Japanese. Before he was shot down and captured by the Japanese, Boyington downed 28 enemy planes. He, too, won the Medal of Honor.

+ Major Gregory "Pappy" Boyington

ISLAND-HOPPING STRATEGY

The Japanese strategy of conquest was to seize islands in the Pacific and reinforce them with airfields, squadrons, and strong defensive fortifications. These island outposts would thus be strong enough to both intercept any American fleet that sailed within reach of its planes and defend itself against any direct attack.

The American high command realized that an attempt to attack and conquer all those island "fortresses" would cause the war to easily last 10 years or more and would cost the lives of hundreds of thousands of men. That just wouldn't do.

Fortunately, Japan did not have the resources to fortify every island. As a result, the Americans created an island-hopping strategy. They would bypass and isolate the islands that had the strongest Japanese garrisons by seizing and fortifying other, more weakly held islands. Once the Americans had conquered an island, they would quickly build an airfield, and use air power to intercept any Japanese counter-attack and to protect the American forces in their leapfrog assault on the next island.

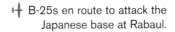 B-25s en route to attack the Japanese base at Rabaul.

THE GREAT MARIANAS TURKEY SHOOT

✛ A Japanese plane is shot down during the Great Marianas Turkey Shoot.

By the middle of 1944, the United States had made huge advances against the Japanese in the Pacific. In the North Pacific, the Japanese had been kicked out of Attu and Kiska in the Aleutians. In the Central Pacific, the outermost island fortresses of Tarawa, Makin, Kwajalein, and Eniwetok had been captured. In the southern Pacific, American forces had liberated the Solomon Islands chain and the large island of New Guinea.

When the Japanese discovered that the Americans were going to try to liberate Saipan, Tinian, and Guam in the Mariana Islands chain in the Central Pacific, they sent the most powerful aircraft-carrier force they could assemble, six carriers and 340 planes, to destroy the U.S. fleet. The U.S. Navy had come a long way since the dark days of early 1942. Now, thanks to the immense manufacturing power of American industry, the U.S. Navy was sailing into battle a total of 15 aircraft carriers that had more than 900 warplanes.

On June 19, 1944, the Battle of the Philippine Sea was fought. It was the greatest carrier battle of the war. When it was over, the Japanese had lost three carriers and virtually all their warplanes while the Americans had lost 130 planes and none of their carriers. Of the aerial dogfights that day, one American Hellcat pilot said, "Why . . . it was just like an old-time turkey shoot back home!" As a result, the battle came to be called the Great Marianas Turkey Shoot.

AIR ATTACKS ON THE JAPANESE HOME ISLANDS: THE B-29 SUPERFORTRESS

With the Marianas now in American hands, the United States had air bases close enough to Japan to begin regular bombing missions on the Japanese home islands. The bomber assigned the task was the largest bomber in the war, the gigantic B-29 Superfortress.

The B-29 was unique among all the bombers because it was the first warplane in the conflict to have a pressurized cabin and remote-control machine-gun turrets.

At first, the B-29s made mostly high-altitude raids on the Japanese cities. But the results were disappointing. Then, in an experiment on March 9, 1945, the B-29s made a low-level night raid on Tokyo, using incendiary bombs. The results were devastating. From that moment on, the B-29s switched to mostly incendiary missions. Major cities were virtually wiped out by the resulting firestorms. The B-29s would continue the missions up until the time of the dropping of the atomic bombs.

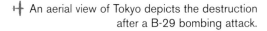 An aerial view of Tokyo depicts the destruction after a B-29 bombing attack.

U.S. ARMY AIR FORCE ACES IN THE PACIFIC

The two greatest aces in World War II flew for the USAAF and fought in the Pacific Theater of Operations (PTO). They were Major Richard Ira Bong and Major Tommy McGuire. Both men were awarded the Medal of Honor.

Major Richard Ira Bong

Major Bong almost didn't make it into the war. While he was still training in California, he couldn't resist looping the loop around the center span of the Golden Gate Bridge in San Francisco with his P-38. Unfortunately for him, his commanding officer heard about it. Bong was lucky that all he got was a reprimand. Bong proved to be a great leader, as well as an excellent fighter pilot. At the war's end, Bong was America's top ace, with a confirmed 40 enemy planes shot down.

✠ Richard Ira Bong

Major Thomas B. McGuire Jr.

Major McGuire was America's second-highest-scoring ace with 38 confirmed enemy planes shot down. He was loved by his fellow pilots. McGuire died over the Philippines shortly after scoring his 38th kill. During an attempt to rescue a fellow pilot who had been jumped by Japanese planes, McGuire's P-38 stalled and crashed into the jungle.

KAMIKAZES

As 1944 began, it was clear to the Japanese high command that unless they did something desperate, they would lose the war. In February 1944, staff officers began exploring the possibility of creating special suicide squadrons, called kamikazes, or "divine wind," that would deliberately fly their bomb-laden planes into American targets.

Organized by Vice Admiral Takijiro Onishi, the Kamikaze Special Attack Corps launched its first mission in October 1944 against escort aircraft carriers in the Battle of Leyte Gulf.

Japanese pilots eagerly volunteered to be kamikazes. They believed that if they died in the act of damaging or destroying an enemy ship, they had performed the greatest duty possible for their country. One pilot, Lieutenant Shigeyuki Suzuki, wrote: "The great day that we can directly be in contact with the battle is our day of happiness and at the same time, the memorial of our death."

Vice Admiral Onishi composed a poem about the kamikazes:

> *In blossom today, then scattered:*
> *Life is so like a delicate flower.*
> *How can one expect the fragrance*
> *To last forever?*

Kamikaze attacks continued until the end of the war. The worst attacks came during the American invasion of the island of Okinawa. These demonstrated the determination of the Japanese to fight to the finish and helped influence the decision to drop the atomic bombs.

✠ The crew of the carrier USS *Bunker Hill* battles a fire caused by a kamikaze attack.

THE ATOMIC BOMB: HIROSHIMA AND NAGASAKI

By the summer of 1945, Japan was isolated. Okinawa, an island virtually at Japan's doorstep, had been conquered by the Americans. The war in Europe had ended with Germany's surrender in May of that year. Now the full might of the Allies could be focused on Japan.

Pilot Paul W. Tibbets

Invasion plans were made, but the United States estimated that it would suffer a million casualties in the assault. This deeply concerned President Harry S Truman, who had become president upon the death of Franklin Roosevelt on April 12, 1945. If there were any way he could avoid such American bloodshed, he vowed to do it. He had a way that might work. It was a new, recently tested explosive device called the atomic bomb. Reports claimed that one bomb could level a large city. President Truman ordered that the bomb be dropped. It was hoped that the destruction caused by the atomic bomb would cause the Japanese leaders to surrender.

On August 6, 1945, history was again made by air power. On that day, the B-29 Superfortress *Enola Gay*, piloted by Colonel Paul W. Tibbets, took off from Tinian Island. In the B-29's bomb bay was one bomb, the atomic bomb nicknamed "Little Boy."

At 8:16 A.M., that atomic bomb was dropped on Hiroshima, Japan. The explosion leveled large parts of the city, and the atomic bomb's signature mushroom cloud became a new symbol of war's destruction.

The *Enola Gay* lands after dropping the first atomic bomb on Hiroshima, Japan, August 6, 1945.

Because the Japanese government did not respond to the Allies' demand to surrender, a second atomic bomb, nicknamed "Fat Boy," carried by the B-29 *Bock's Car*, piloted by Major Charles Sweeney, was dropped on Nagasaki on August 9. When the mushroom cloud over Nagasaki blew away, another Japanese city had been leveled.

With the destruction of Nagasaki, the Japanese government capitulated and signed the terms of surrender on the U.S. battleship *Missouri* on September 2, 1945. Thanks to the use of air power, countless American lives were saved, and World War II was over.

(opposite): The atomic bomb mushroom cloud rises above Hiroshima.

GLOSSARY

Allies—The name for the nations, primarily Great Britain, the United States, the Soviet Union, and France, united against the Axis powers.

Axis—The countries, primarily Germany, Italy, and Japan, that fought against the Allies.

Blitzkrieg—The German word for "lightning war." A swift, overpowering military offensive of combined land and air forces led by tanks and other armored vehicles.

Campaign—A series of major military operations designed to achieve a long-range goal.

Capitulation—An agreement of surrender.

D-Day—Literally "Day-Day." Originally the code name for the day on which a military offensive is to be launched. Specifically refers to June 6, 1944, the Allied invasion of Normandy, France.

Dive-bomber—Warplanes that attack their targets by flying toward them at a steep angle prior to the release of their explosives.

Garrison—A military post or a group of troops stationed at a particular location.

Gliders—In World War II, an engine-less aircraft used to transport airborne troops and supplies to battle.

Kamikaze—The Japanese word for "divine wind." In World War II, the term described Japanese pilots trained to make suicide attacks on enemy targets, usually warships, with their warplanes.

Luftwaffe—The German Air Force.

Medal of Honor—The highest military decoration awarded in the United States to all branches for gallantry and bravery above and beyond the call of duty in action against the enemy.

Nazi—The acronym for NAtionalsoZIalist, the first word of the official title of Hitler's political party, the Nationalsozialistische Deutsche Arbeiterpartie or NSDAP (National Socialist German Workers' Party).

Panzer—The German term for "armor." In World War II, *Panzerwagen*, or tank, was shortened to Panzer.

Soviet Union—From 1917–1991, the nation known officially as the Union of Soviet Socialist Republics; a nation containing 15 communist-governed republics and dominated by its largest republic, Russia.

Theater—The large geographical area where military operations are coordinated.

INDEX